HUNGARY

Text	Earleen Brunner
Photography	Claude Huber
Design	Robert Rausis

Berlitz Trademark Reg. U.S. Patent Office
and other countries – Marca Registrada.

Library of Congress Catalog
Card No. 83-082005

Printed in Switzerland by Weber S.A., Bienne.

HUNGARY

EDITIONS BERLITZ

A DIVISION OF MACMILLAN S.A.

Introduction

This book charts a journey, my journey to Hungary, a trip that took me the length and breadth of the land. I came in search of a country, a people, a tradition a thousand years old. For Hungary is ancient, enduring, resilient even. Through a long and difficult history, Hungary has held fast to its inscrutable language, its national identity, its pride.

But first, before there was a Hungary, there was the land: sweeping plains, a narrow spine of mountains, a network of rivers and lakes. Then came the people: Árpád, Magyar chieftain, the horsemen in his train. Out of seven tribes was forged one body, one nation—the Hungary of Stephen, first king and confessor. Settlements, monasteries, cities grew up and flourished, only to be laid waste; for the Mongols advanced, looting, pillaging, burning. Not a brick was left standing. Béla IV began the rebuilding. A golden age dawned, the age of Matthias Corvinus, humanist king, Renaissance man. It was not to last; the Turks attacked and conquered, ushering in a century and a half of Ottoman rule. The Habsburgs freed Hungary and imposed a new suit and service. Revolts flared up; the Habsburgs kept power. Freedom came late, in the twentieth century. Hungary survived to emerge as an Eastern European state, the People's Republic of Hungary.

Hungary has all the monuments a momentous past provides—Gothic town houses, Baroque palaces, Neo-classical cathedrals. Some have withstood the ravages of war; others have been restored. Hungary also has a folklore renowned for its richness. Traditional customs and beliefs linger on, perpetuated by villagers in thousands of rural communities. Hungary has a distinctive cuisine. Manifold sports possibilities. Awesome landscapes. And its people. Nothing about Hungary impressed me more than the people. Spirited, independent, fiercely patriotic, they are attached to the very idea of Hungary and to the land itself.

4

Time and time again, I listened as Hungarians expressed their love of country. No other place is ever quite like Hungary. Or so a man of Kecskemét told me. An expatriate living in Germany, he returned to his native city after a traumatic divorce. He could think of nothing but "going home", he said. And then there was the woman who had spent many years in Canada. Left alone after the death of her husband and the marriage of her daughter, she felt "homesick" for Budapest and her old friends. Of course she missed her daughter and her grandchild, but life sometimes demands difficult choices. She had made her decision, and she was happy—speaking her language, eating Hungarian bread (a bread like no other bread, she assured me), breathing Hungarian air. A young man, an artist, had another tale of exodus and return. After some time abroad, he had taken up residence in Sopron—"the most beautiful city in the world"—to be near his ageing parents. They needed him, he needed them—and Sopron. A country-music singer, József Kovács by name, tried to explain, in English, how he felt about Hungary. He occasionally makes foreign tours, and he always looks forward to the trips. But he is never completely at ease away from home. Hungary inspires him. Hungary is his life. "Hungary … mine", he said, searching in his mind for the proper verb.

Earleen Brunner
Senior Editor
Editions Berlitz

LAND

Majestic, fast-flowing, the Danube surges through the heart of Hungary, providing water in a land of grass. Without the Danube there would be no Hungary. Along the Czechoslovak frontier, scores of alluvial islands lie in its path. But the river moves ever eastward, narrowing and gathering force as it cuts through the Visegrád hills, dividing to hold the cathedral city of Esztergom in a sinuous embrace. It negotiates the historic Danube Bend, looping narrowly at Visegrád to continue on a southerly course. Ancient trees bend into the water at the site of King Matthias's ruined palace, but the ramparts of stone hold little magic for me. I see only the Danube, snaking through steeply plunging hills, hazy in the late afternoon light.

Divided again by the green tongue of Szentendre Island, the river glides past the landing stage of Vác, long a strategic crossing point, and on to Szentendre on the opposite shore. Cobbled lanes lead from the waterfront to the centre of town, out of sight at Marx Square. Turning away from the river and the twentieth century too, Szentendre preserves the aura of Habsburg Hungary in street after street of old Baroque houses, thick with stucco decoration, vivid paintwork weathered by the sun.

With Budapest just downriver, the Danube courses on through a changing scene of high-rise flats and industrial buildings. Canoes, kayaks and rowing-boats join the flow of river traffic, and fishermen gather here and there along the banks. The river is at its most grandiose as it enters the capital, dividing historic Buda from Pest, the commercial quarter. It sweeps through in a wide arc, echoed by the concentric boulevards of Pest. The cardinal point is Elizabeth Bridge, site ten centuries ago of the city's first landing stage. Imposing public buildings flank the Pest embankment—the immense Neo-gothic Parliament, Academy of Science, Inner City Parish Church and Vigadó—as well as a clutch of glass-and-steel hotels. They're situated on the Korzó, a once-fashionable waterfront promenade, now restored to the city. But the life of

7

the river isn't to be found here, however spectacular the panorama. I sense it only as I wander the embankments, where the same old men come day after day to fish for pike and carp, where captains call to one another as they tinker with their boats, where you can see the tide swell and the light slant on the oily surface of the Danube.

Beyond the city the river forms two arms, which join again near the new town of Dunaújváros. And on it flows, south to the Yugoslav border, marking as it goes the divide between two great regions, Transdanubia to the west and the Great Plain to the east. The Danube carries traffic through eight countries, from Germany to the Black Sea, but it also bears a huge burden of silt that darkens the waters and interferes with navigation channels. The river seems eternal, immutable, yet its contours shift imperceptibly every day, as one bank erodes and another is built up.

Nowhere is the Danube more capricious than in the Forest of Gemenc—a nature preserve extending for twenty miles along the southern reaches of the Danube. Here the river breaks its bonds, erupting at every turn into serpentine meanders. Fishermen haunt the backwaters, casting close to shore from small, flat-bottomed boats held fast against the drift of the current. Like fishermen everywhere, they sit motionless for hours, lost in thought, contemplating nothing more than the eddying current and nothing less than time and the river.

And all around is the Gemenc. Rare waterfowl like the osprey and black stork nest on the banks of the Danube and its offshoots, and heron wade in the shallows. Willows overhang the water and there are aspens, too. Away from the river stretches a fantastical forest, dark, deep and impenetrable. This is the dwelling place of deer and wild boar, an enchanted wood where the cuckoo calls. A rustle of leaves announces the approach of a boar, but there is nothing to fear, it would appear. The animal attacks only when injured, though a female will face down an intruder to protect her young.

I learn that boars in the Gemenc feed on snails and insects (in plentiful supply), fish bones, dead animals and picnickers' remains. I look in vain for a herd of deer, antlers held high, but the deer is a more elusive creature and keeps to its secret lair. Beyond the protected zone, week-end houses cluster on the edge of the forest. Most of them are modest and some frankly makeshift, but none more incongruous than an old bus, its vintage paintwork going to rust, trellised lovingly with roses. Almost every Hungarian has a home away from home it seems.

The Danube rushes past the old river port of Baja and on across the border. While far away in the Nyírség—an intensively cultivated region

8

The river breaks its bonds,
erupting at every turn into
serpentine meanders.

Fishermen haunt the backwaters, casting close to shore from small, flat-bottomed boats.

bordering on the Soviet Union—Hungary's second river begins the long journey south to Yugoslavia. Eulogized by the poet Sándor Petőfi as the "wild Tisza", "our Tisza", it winds down to the wine town of Tokaj and industrial Leninváros and on through the Great Plain. Vignettes of rural life unfold at every turn: a man takes up a hoe, a woman draws water from a well, cows graze placidly.... The Tisza pursues a longer and more circuitous course than the Danube, though many of the twists and turns have been eliminated to reclaim land for cultivation. Once violent and prone to severe flooding, it has been tamed by an extensive system of dikes ever in evidence on the Great Plain. And it was on the Great Plain, heading towards Hortobágy, that I had my first sight of the Tisza: languorous, expansive, as wide as the plain itself in places. It is hard to believe that such peaceable waters ever had the potential to "swallow up the whole world", as Petőfi put it.

Before regulation, the flood waters of the Tisza streamed over the Hortobágy, the vast prairie that lies east of the river. Land was cultivated and farming villages flourished. Originally all was meadow and virgin forest, but the Turks destroyed the trees and dispersed the population. And so the puszta was created—the barren steppe that is Hungary's most austere landscape. The very name means "bleak". Tens of thousands of acres in the heart of the puszta form a national park where rare migratory birds are protected and the unique animals of Hungary are bred: the *nónius* horse, so wide of chest, the Hungarian grey bull and a kind of long-haired sheep with corkscrew horns known as the *racka*. Since irrigation was introduced thirty years ago or more, agriculture has made a vigorous comeback beyond the conservation zone.

The park directorate and agricultural enterprises have administrative headquarters in Hortobágy village, where tourism comes into its own. The eighteenth-century *csárda,* or inn, has been renovated to accommodate large groups of visitors, and there are no less than three museums and a horse-ring where tourist spectacles are staged. I could have occupied myself nicely without actually venturing into the puszta. Yet the village does, after all, belong to the Great Plain. There are silent midnights canopied with stars and dawns noisy with the din of labourers setting off for work in the rice fields or on one model farm or another. I needn't have been dismayed by the tourist phenomenon. There is no escaping the limitless puszta.

It takes time to adjust to the landscape—to the relentless sweep of sky and the apparent monotony of the terrain. Up close, that flat, flat plain proves alarmingly uneven; enormous troughs loom up out of nowhere,

14

The Danube carries traffic through eight countries, from Germany to the Black Sea.

and the ground can be unyielding one minute, soft and spongy the next. Vestigial thickets of acacia trees heave into sight now and then—oases of green in a sea of tawny grass. And the grass itself is infinitely variegated, flecked with russet and gold, scattered over with flowers—stretching off to the farthest horizon in alternating bands of colour.

No one would dream of striking out in the puszta on foot. There are neither paved roads nor footpaths: even dirt tracks are few and far between. A horse is the favoured mode of transport here. As for vehicles, only a jeep or cart can withstand the brutal punishment inflicted by such rough territory. Ensconced in a cart of my own—a traditional one with heavy wooden wheels and spindle decoration—I jostle cross-country, absorbed in the immensity of the puszta, moving slowly, ever so slowly.

Several hundred *nónius* horses have the run of all this pastureland. They are bred mainly to preserve the strain—developed to carry cannon during the Napoleonic wars—but also for racing. These horses thrive in the *szik*, the dry alkali plain, and are known properly as the *sziki nónius*. István Zilahy, trainer of the Hortobágy State Horse Farm, explains that the animals graze from four o'clock in the morning until eight or nine at night, herded by several men working together. The rest of the time, they are stabled in long, low thatched buildings on the edge of the puszta. I watch as part of the herd thunders past, sleek and wild and free: one man can control dozens of animals with a crack of his whip. Horseherds, known as *csikós,* wear traditional wide-legged trousers, shirt and waistcoat, with a broad-brimmed black felt hat. István points out that they are required to do so. A herdsman named Lajos claims to like the outfit, and he demonstrates the practicality of the headgear in all weathers, turning down the protective brim. Fit and middle-aged, content withal, Lajos knows no life other than that of the plain. He sits lightly in his saddle—and that is no small matter, for the Hungarian variety has no girth; it rests on the horse, no more.

In motion again, slow motion again, I roll on across the interminable plain that conceals nothing and everything. A cowherd appears just ahead, materializing out of thin air. Had he been there all the time, I wondered? This is no apparition, however, but the guardian of Hungarian greys. The Hortobágy supports a sizeable herd of around a thousand animals. Legend has it that the first Magyars introduced the breed into the country in the tenth century. Whatever their pedigree, the greys are intimidating—especially the bulls with their long horns tipped in copper. I look around for protection from that massive flesh, those powerful hooves, but the old cowherd is dispassionate. He leans on his stick and

Hungary is ancient, enduring, resilient even.

17

talks about himself. Like the other men who work on the puszta, he lives mainly in the company of herders, seeing little of his family. Times have changed; he has television and radio and an engine for his well. But he still spends long hours on the plain, alone with the cattle. He shows me how he keeps the Hungarian greys in line, sending his *komondor* to snap at their hooves, indicating the direction the dog should go with his stick. Standing there in his coarse herdsman's trousers, baggy in the thigh and tight in the leg, he seems as much a part of the landscape as the wells with their towering sweep poles, or the Hungarian greys themselves.

The long-haired *racka* graze in a distant locale. The sheep dart back and forth in unison through the tall grass, brandishing the prodigious spirals of their horns. The shepherds of old lived almost entirely from the meat of this unique breed, brought to Hungary by the Magyars a thousand years ago. Now no more than half a dozen shepherds, or *juhász*, are left in the Hortobágy, and no more than two or three thousand sheep. The flock scatters as I approach, and a fat shepherd lumbers up, followed by his *komondor*. He's a young man, and in his twill work trousers and battered beret, he could be a factory worker or a mechanic—but for his staff and his sense of vocation.

The Hortobágy is the site of goose-breeding, too. I cross another vast stretch of puszta to see the birds for myself. The cart bounces along and I am lost on the plain again, only to be brought up short by the ululating cries of five thousand geese, grazing together. The birds are raised for their meat and liver, as well as for their feathers, which they produce generously, three times a year. A bevy of workers does the plucking by hand. Nowadays goose-breeding is an industry, not a life's occupation. It was never a glamorous job in any case. In the old hierarchy of the plain, the gooseherd came last, after the cowherd and shepherd. The horseherd lorded it over them all. But the most romantic figure was the *betyár*, the outlaw, on the run for theft or worse. Expert riders all, outlaws could outdistance any pursuer. The herdsmen idolized them and the puszta gave them shelter. For the puszta has always been a world apart and a law unto itself.

And on the periphery of this world are *tanyák*, smallholdings that were carved from the plain in the centuries after the Turkish occupation. Peasant families still lead isolated but independent lives here, calling no man master. Near Bugac, towards the southern extremity of the Great Plain, a peasant invites me onto land his family has worked for more than two hundred years. The fields of corn and wheat, the orchard, vineyard and vegetable garden are a whole universe to him, and life begins and

Geese are raised for their meat and liver, as well as for their feathers.

Before there was a Hungary there
was the land.

ends in the thatched farmhouse where he was born. All a man needs to make him happy, I speculate, are two cows and a horse and a cellar stocked with his own wine, beer and brandy. All the same, the future of the *tanya* is uncertain; the farmer's son and daughter have deserted the country to work in town.

Many *tanyák* lie abandoned. New uses have been found for many more. I spend a night and a day on a *tanya* bordering on the duneland of Bugac. The farmhouse has been converted into a hotel, a simple place owned and managed by one János Varga of Kecskemét, a television repairman by trade. His all-consuming passion is collecting folk art objects. The sheepskin coats, gas lamps, pottery and other pieces he has acquired (mostly in the line of duty, he says) are on display all over the farmhouse, which is itself a relic of peasant architecture. More important still, the *tanya* forms part of that evocative entity, the puszta. Like the pampas for the Argentinian and the Far West for the American, the puszta looms large in the Hungarian popular imagination. Here Varga comes to renew himself and here he will live when he can afford to do so.

Itinerant beekeepers set up their hives all through the rolling countryside.

Bugac lies within the boundaries of Kiskunság National Park, the counterpart of the Hortobágy, with its own tourist shows, museum and old inn. The same flat wastes extend far and wide, but there are also vast stretches of sand, heaped into hills and drifting, drifting. Clumps of grass grow knee-high in places, binding the sand, and juniper trees flourish. So do vipers and rabbits. I set off on foot to see the duneland at close range, strolling casually along a boardwalk raised just above the undulating sandy steppe. The walkway ends all too soon at the foot of a hill of sand. I struggle up one side and down the next, and on and on over hill after hill. Surely the Sahara itself has no more sand than this. I long for the shade of a juniper but abandon the idea when a lizard, small, inoffensive and green as grass, reminds me that vipers may well lurk here. Later, not far from the park, I see a peasant woman from a neighbouring *tanya* pedalling laboriously through the sand on a bicycle, completely at home in this inhospitable land.

If the puszta is Hungary's desert, then the Balaton is its sea—an inland sea of liquid silver, ringed round with hills. Villas, holiday flats and resort hotels sweep unremittingly along the lakeshore from Balatonaliga to Balatonberény. I'm never quite sure where one town ends and the next begins, they merge into each other so neatly. Though rain threatens, people in beach gear throng the lakeside road, determined to make the most of the day. The beach, after all, is wide and sandy and the shallow lake waters are warm. I take the ferry from Szántód to Tihany—the

22

Peasant families lead isolated
but independent lives here.

wooded peninsula that comes within half a mile of the south shore. A cover of clouds hangs over the lake, and the air lies heavy and cool on the metallic surface of the water. In ten minutes, no more, I reach Tihany harbour.

An ancient centre of Christianity, Tihany has a historic old abbey church. There are fishermen's houses of white stucco and thatch and ochre-painted holiday villas. A tree-lined promenade parallels the lakeshore, and wherever you look you see the carmine of roses. Tihany is also a nature conservation area with volcanic hills, hot water springs and a curious little inner lake choked with reeds and rife with fishermen. It lies on a plateau well above the level of the Balaton. The scent of lavender and wild thyme hangs in the air and sunflowers turn in the wind. Corn fields, wheat fields and vineyards fan out across the peninsula and beyond—all along the northern shore and up into the Bakony Mountains. Wine cellars slope into the hillsides wherever there are vines.

The century-old cellars of Aszófő, a village at the head of the peninsula, look like small shrines to the god of wine, with their ornate stucco façades and steeply pitched roofs; grassy tumuli cover the deep, dim storerooms. Though Csopak's cellars are simpler affairs, Csopak wines enjoy immemorial renown. A doctor of the village, near Balatonfüred, offers to open his cellar. He uses heavy iron keys massive enough to unlock the very gates of paradise. And so they do. I inspect the winepress—an infernal, hand-cranked machine—and continue on into the storeroom where rows of wooden barrels are ranged. Each contains a different wine, blended by the doctor according to old family methods. With the traditional glass *borlopó*, he siphons off half a dozen whites made from varying proportions of Rizling and Muscat Ottonel grapes. The wine is fresh, volatile, elusive. It is tinged with sweetness—and with the sadness of evanescent pleasures. I drink and drink again as we sit out in the vineyard, our feet planted in the soil of Csopak, savouring the fellowship of wine.

No one understood the Balaton better than József Egry, first painter of the region. Cured of a grave illness at Keszthely during the Great War, he went on to live permanently at Badacsony, in sight of the lake. The Balaton was Egry's Mont Sainte-Victoire, and like Cézanne with the mountain, he always saw it anew. Egry limned the Balaton at all hours and in all weathers. He produced scene after scene of flatboats and sailboats, of fishermen and reeds, of spectral figures staring out at the lake from hilltops, docks and quaysides, of sunlight streaming down eternally on his beloved Balaton.

The wide arc of the Bakony Mountains follows the sweep of the lake, protecting it from the winds that blow off the Alps. They say the climate is harsh, with much snow and rain, but I find a gentler reality: green hills and golden fields lie in the first flush of summer, caressed by the warming sun. A century ago and more, the Bakony was thick with trees and devoid of people—save for the woodcutter (that legendary raconteur) and swineherd, whose pigs grew fat on acorns in the oak forests. Outlaws fled here, too. Apart from the puszta, no other area offered so many possibilities for seclusion. People still talk about Józsi Savanyú, who went to earth in a cave near Badacsonyszentlászló, completely and utterly beyond capture. The way they tell it, you'd think it had happened yesterday. Yet time has passed, without a doubt: I look up at Csesznek, seven centuries old, and the castle crumbles into ruins before my eyes.

A spine of mountains extends all across the north of Hungary: the Pilis range, the Cserhát, the Bükk, Mátra and Zemplén. The slopes are variously forested, terraced with vineyards or blanketed with lavender and the yellow of mustard. Itinerant beekeepers set up their hives all through the rolling countryside, transporting them in big vans. On the road in the Pilis Mountains, I hail a man who is gathering pollen. Around him lie fields that were once a favourite hunting ground of Hungarian royalty. He offers me a net-swathed hat as bees swarm menacingly, and we begin to talk. He tells me he likes the work: the season is short and the money is good. He enjoys moving from place to place and his wife often comes with him to help out with the bees. Keeping bees is no more than a pleasant sideline for him, albeit a profitable one; officially he earns his living as a carpenter. It's a good life, he says, flashing a toothless smile.

On a hilltop in the Pilis uplands, the broken towers of Zsámbék thrust against the sky. Swallows nest in the Romanesque masonry of this monastery church, destroyed by earthquake two centuries past. Scoured by wind and weather, the church seems a natural outgrowth of the grassy summit on which it stands. All the arches are shattered, save for one perfect span, and the roof and north wall have fallen away altogether. Once the work of man, Zsámbék has been claimed irrevocably by the forces of nature.

Trees shade the road that winds through the Cserhát, a richly agricultural region planted with wheat, corn and potatoes. Roadside vendors sell tender heads of lettuce and crimson tomatoes. Women in traditional pleated skirts and puff-sleeved blouses cycle past, their backbaskets overflowing with vegetables. Men wear work clothes and carry hoes. They are *palócok*, members of an ethnic minority set apart by their dialect and dress. Alongside venerable white stucco houses with columned verandahs are houses no older than the century; they have tile roofs and gingerbread carving. Wells with chains and cranks stand in front yards and poppies run riot.

Further east, oak trees tower above the heights of the Mátra range (a spa and sports centre), while vineyards in serried ranks progress across the lower slopes. Coming into the market town of Gyöngyös, I pass cellars where much of the wine is pressed and stored. There seem to be hundreds of them, set one after another into the limestone slopes that extend down to the roadway. Heavy wooden portals flush with the rock face close on the thousand and one delights of the caverns within.

The Mátra gives way to the Bükk chain, and Eger lies in between. Wrapped in leafy trees and cool mountain air, the town seems almost alpine. I forego visits to the fortress and minaret to sit in a shady garden, drinking tonic draughts of *Egri Bikavér*, Bull's Blood of Eger, the wine that seduced a pasha. For tradition has it that one year during the Turkish occupation, the people of Eger offered their pasha *Egri Bikavér* in payment for taxes. The crops had failed and they had nothing else of value to give him. This put the pasha, a devout Muslim, into a dilemma: though alcohol was forbidden him, he had great difficulty resisting the captivating bouquet of the dark, velvety wine. A neat solution was found when he declared that the wine was indeed the blood of bulls and so could drink it in good conscience.

The most famous wine-growing region of all is Tokaj, east again in the foothills of the Zemplén Mountains. This is the native heath of sweet *Tokaji aszu* and the semi-sweet *Szamorodni,* celebrated for long centuries by kings and courtiers, poets and patricians. The vines hug the hillsides, rooted deep in the volcanic soil, absorbing the fire, the spirit, the very essence of Hungary's good earth.

The Gemenc is the dwelling place of deer and wild boar, an enchanted wood where the cuckoo calls.

It was on the Great Plain that
I had my first sight of the Tisza:
languorous, expansive, as wide
as the plain itself in places.

LIFE

Remote and dreamy in the last light of day, Budapest is a mythical city, a place I've imagined and not real at all. From my vantage point high on Gellért Hill, the impossible bulk of Parliament seems to levitate above the Danube and the river itself looks dim and glassy. Margaret Island is reduced to a haze of trees and every spire of every church hovers in the darkling sky. Hungary has other cities, but there is only one Buda, one Pest, one capital city of Budapest.

Mansions medieval and Baroque crowd the narrow, cobbled streets of Buda's Castle District, a romantic enclave on a little plateau overlooking the river. I like the gentle air of decrepitude, the faded brilliance of the paintwork and the plaster flaking from the walls—the sense of time having passed. Beethoven lived here and Thomas Mann, too. Nowadays some of the houses shelter museums, but most are still tenanted: an old man, book in hand, peers down at me from an open window, and a woman looks up as she weeds the patch of garden in front of her house. No one seems to mind the fact that people throng the area. Tourists converge above all on Szentháromság Square, site of Matthias Church, a confection of lustrous tile and Neo-gothic tracery. Alongside is the Budapest Hilton, a landmark construction of glass, steel and historic stone, rising on venerable foundations. The turreted promenade of whimsical Fishermen's Bastion revives the Romanesque style. But a more sober architect had his way with the Royal Palace, further along, interesting mainly for the museums it contains.

I seek out the relics of Hungary's fifteenth-century golden age, when Matthias Corvinus was king. It was a fleeting period and little in the way of monuments remains, for the Turks destroyed almost everything in their wake. One important vestige is the Hercules Fountain from Visegrád Palace, which I spy stranded on a landing at the National Gallery. Out of context, it looks like a replica at first glance. But this is indeed the marble well that gushed red wine and white at royal banquets, alternately and

Half of all Hungarians live in towns, and of that half, nearly half again reside in Budapest.

endlessly they say. The well bears the insignia of the king, surrounded by garlands of flowers—a hallmark of the Renaissance style that Matthias favoured, alone of all the monarchs north of the Alps.

The remains of Matthias's Buda Palace on display at the Museum of History make more of an impact. The most sculpturesque and imposing of fragments seem to have survived: ceiling panels, portals of marble and friezes carved with the gods and goddesses of classical myth, with dolphins and with perfect little cherubs, their faces framed with curls. Hungary did indeed experience a Renaissance, that much is clear. The ideals of Italian humanism and the art that expressed those ideals took hold here earlier—and more authentically—than anywhere else in the world. I think of what might have been, had it not been for the Turks, and the occupation, a century and a half long, gains new significance.

I leave the confines of the Castle District for the cosmopolite attractions of Pest, crossing town by taxi. Not just any taxi, but a taxi whose driver has clocked 500,000 kilometres accident free. Displayed on the dashboard is the medal to prove it, engraved with the wreath and star of the People's Republic. Medal or no, I hold on tight as we swoop through the traffic at breakneck speed, careening past Rudas Baths—a mecca of steam and sulphur for four hundred years—and onto the Chain Bridge, the first to span the Danube. Ahead stretch the boulevards of Pest, a kaleidoscope of granite and grisaille. Built with elegant old apartment blocks and offices, these wide avenues exude all the confidence of the Belle Epoque, all the worldliness of the twenties, when writers and artists were drawn to Budapest, "Little Paris on the Danube". I hear literary figures still gather at the Hungária, a century-old café in Nagykörút—and that may well be. I have the plush, the mirrors, the marble to myself. I take my coffee in the company of shades, haunted by the spectre of Attila József, Hungary's great revolutionary poet, a café regular. Impoverished and in ill health, he died, a suicide at the age of thirty-two, "Without father without mother, Without god and homeland either...". It is strange to think of that tragic figure in these gilded surroundings, where Josephine Baker, Emil Jannings and Mistinguett rubbed shoulders with Maurice Ravel and Spain's King Alfonso.

Cradled within the sweep of the boulevards is the ancient quarter of Pest, the throbbing inner city, centred on Váci Street, Petőfi Street, Kigyó and Régiposta streets. These streets were made for walking and that is what I do, pausing now and then to look in the shops. There are small outlets for records, clothing, arts and crafts, food and wine. There are state-run department stores and private boutiques—small enterprises that represent a burgeoning sector of the Hungarian economy. For Hungary has a thriving fashion industry and many talented designers. An abundance of hairdressers and beauticians ministers to the public, and the manicurists and pedicurists of the inner city announce their services on mirrored signs decorated with evocative images of perfect hands and feet. A few antique dealers have premises here, but I prefer the flea market on the eastern outskirts of the city.

Crowded with merchants and market regulars, the long aisles of the covered section are strewn with gas lamps, vintage phonographs and tattered silk umbrellas. Every article is consecrated by long use and the patina of time: clocks without movements, watches without hands, gold rings, glass jugs and oil paintings of uncertain provenance, undated, unsigned. The inner workings of a hundred different machines occupy an area apart: nuts, screws and bolts, wires, flexes and tubing have all been sorted into orderly piles by some methodical hand. Outdoors, worn carpets are stacked perilously high and dilapidated armchairs and tottery chests huddle together, helter-skelter. Food vendors do a rushing auxiliary trade in coffee, cola and sausage snacks. After some deliberation, I make off with an accordion-pleated peasant skirt, sprigged with flowers. Even though you don't bargain for the price, a kind of complicity accompanies transactions.

Yet people seem to buy nothing so much as books. It is Book Week, a twice-yearly promotion of new titles, and stands piled with books line Váci Street, spilling over into Vörösmarty Square. Authors are on hand to autograph their works, and long queues form at every stand and in front of all the bookshops in the area. At a pavement stand in Kálvin Square, the Reformed Church offers devotional titles for sale. Books with art-related themes are displayed in museums. Clearly Hungary is a nation of readers.

Many here are religious, too, something I discover quite by chance. Lost and wandering aimlessly around Engels Square, I ask directions of a man, a Catholic as it turns out. He shows me the way, insisting all the while that I must also look in on the Basilica nearby, trying desperately hard to convince me that a momentous event is to take place. And so I go along to the church, the century-old Parish Church of St. Stephen, where thousands of people are gathered and thousands more arrive—filling to overflowing that echoing interior, so sepulchral, so vast. They are waiting for a service of commemoration to begin, a service held once in a century: it is the thirtieth of May, and Hungary's great Christian king, Stephen I, was sanctified nine hundred years ago to the day.

46

The river is at its most grandiose as it enters the capital, dividing historic Buda from Pest, the commercial quarter.

The altar is ablaze with candles and light pours down on the white marble image of the saint. Priests and acolytes sit off to one side, guarding that most precious relic of the Hungarian church, Stephen's right hand, known as the Holy Right. Sealed in an illuminated casket of gilt and glass, it is shown to the faithful but once every hundred years, on the day of Stephen's sanctification. Every eye follows as the hand is taken up and displayed to the congregation in a procession that winds solemnly around the sanctuary. Flags are held high, the flags of Hungary and of the royal house of Árpád, of the Basilica and of the Christian church. Hungary's archbishop arrives, and the songs of the holy service ring out in Latin and in Hungarian. One anthem recalls four saints of Hungary: Stephen or István, Imre, László, Gellért. The depth of emotion that this hymn evokes is practically tangible. Tears pour down the face of the man standing alongside me; many women weep. The refrain implores God not to forget "poor Hungary". It is a kind of national anthem, a sincere expression of faith in God and love of country. In the Hungary of today, neither sentiment goes amiss.

St. Stephen's hand may belong to the church, but his crown is the possession of the state—the very crown Stephen wore on Christmas Day in the year 1000, when he was anointed king. Hungary has no more potent symbol of nationhood than this golden diadem, heavy with jewels and rich with enamelling. On a rainy Sunday afternoon, I watch as Hungarians stream into the National Museum's room of royal regalia. They speak reverently, in whispers, their attention never deflected for a moment from the royal crown. Not for them the passing curiosity of a tourist: they look long and hard at their greatest national treasure, an ineffable piece of history, the embodiment of a thousand years of striving and of pride.

But Budapest has other symbols, other monuments, other landmarks, each telling in its own way. There is the ruin of Aquincum, that outpost of ancient Rome. And Gül Baba's tomb, a holy shrine of Islam. There is the Millenary Monument to the Magyar conquest, its sublime grandiloquence blunted somewhat by the boundless spaces of Heroes' Square. And the Museum of Fine Arts, fronting on the square. Watched by a phalanx of attendants—old women uniformed in blue—I go from gallery to gallery with cries of recognition, there are so many familiar pictures on display. Fairs and fêtes are held in the grassy confines of City Park, where it always feels like Sunday, whatever the day of the week. Margaret Island is a public park, too, but it lies in the Danube, covered in a mantle of trees. Seven centuries ago, King Béla IV gave his daughter Margaret to God

50

Ahead stretch the boulevards
of Pest, a kaleidoscope of granite
and grisaille.

Hungary has other cities, but
there is only one Buda, one Pest,
one capital city of Budapest.

and to the nuns of the Dominican convent here, and she in turn renounced the world to live out her life on the island that bears her name. For citizens of a modern Budapest, it remains an island of peace, a place of escape.

Half of all Hungarians live in towns, and of that half, nearly half again reside in Budapest. The capital is a magnet for many, but I set out in search of other cities, other realities… Szentendre. I steal quietly into town at six on a Sunday morning. Shafts of sunlight angle down into Marx Square—sunlight as solid, as palpable as the Baroque stonework of the Orthodox church in the square, or the cast-iron filigree of the old Serbian cross. Shut tight against dawn incursions, Szentendre slumbers. There is nothing for it but to wait. At seven, the caretaker of the Catholic Parish Church makes ready for the first mass of the morning. A few people venture out into the streets, and Szentendre slowly stirs to life. The Serbian merchants who settled here after the Turkish occupation gave the town its air of quiet prosperity, its houses of yellow, ochre, rose and green, its Orthodox churches. Outside the Čiprovačka, the Church of Peter and Paul, parishioners lay a carpet of rose petals for Day of the Lord celebrations, which culminate in a procession through nearby streets. Priest and congregation tread slowly along, pausing at altars set up out of doors. Little girls in white scatter flower petals, and members of the congregation—a congregation as diverse as the population of Szentendre itself—sing out together, united by their faith.

By mid-morning, tourists flood into town, into the churches and museums. Szentendre has notable collections of religious and Impressionist art, but the Margit Kovács museum draws the biggest crowds. Margit Kovács was a ceramist renowned in Hungary and abroad. "Clay is my daily bread, my joy and my sorrow", she declared. And out of this joy and sorrow were born the hundreds of pieces on display in Szentendre: statuettes, murals, large figures and pottery vessels. The artist drew inspiration from fairy tale, legend, classical myth and Bible story. From Szentendre's Serbian churches with their onion domes and from the watercolour tints of the houses. Margit Kovács discovered the town in the sixth decade of her life, at a time when her work took on a new depth and heightened expressionism. She lived here until her death in 1977, aged seventy-five, preoccupied with the universal themes of birth, death and old age. Perhaps the most moving piece exhibited in the museum is the rough terracotta of an old daughter embracing an even older mother: *Which is the Mother and Which the Daughter Now?* the artist asks, as she so poignantly depicts the childlike vulnerability of the elderly.

From Szentendre, I go to ancient Esztergom, seat of the primate, Hungary's Rome. The Neo-classical Basilica dominates the town, imposing itself on the skyline by sheer order of magnitude. The cupola is gargantuan, the columns of the porch, colossal. Dwarfed by the immensity of it all, supplicants and sightseers flood across the threshold and into the nave. I follow in their wake, listening as an organist runs up and down the scale at random. The low notes reverberate off the dome like thunder, loud enough to wake Esztergom's erstwhile archbishops, entombed in the crypt. And Cardinal Tamás Bakócz, too, dead four hundred years and more. He lies buried in the chapel that takes his name, built "for the Mother of God, the Blessed Virgin Mary, in the year 1507". It was moved here stone by stone and reassembled, the proof and sum of Hungary's golden age. Cornucopias of fruit and flowers are traced in red marble, and dolphins, and rosettes. Master carvers laboured for twenty years to enrich the last resting place of this powerful churchman, the Hungarian cardinal who nearly became pope.

And in the treasury are precious relics of the see: vestments, chalices, drinking horns, crosses. I crane for a look at the bejewelled Matthias Calvary, an aid to royal devotions; Christ, a sliver of enamel, hangs pinned to a cross of gold. Hungary's medieval kings swore a holy oath on the Coronation Cross, encrusted with pearls and rough-cut precious stones. Enamelwork decorates the gilt Chalice of Benedek Suky, which held the wine of the Eucharist. Scenes from Christ's life and passion crowd the base of the cup and its cumbrous stem, investing this sacred object with the most exalted spiritual meaning.

Esztergom was settled by the Romans. Marcus Aurelius wrote his *Meditations* here. The kings of the house of Árpád ruled from Esztergom. Here St. Stephen was born and crowned king. Here King Matthias's Beatrice lived in the sorrow of her widowhood. But the Mongols and Turks wreaked havoc on the town, and few monuments survive from that glorious past. There is only the royal palace, a ruin, a noble ruin. I wander through passageways, chambers and chapel, ornamented in a patchwork of styles, looking for a thread of continuity in the labyrinthine remains. Fragments of fresco painting cling to powdery walls of brick and bare plaster: a lion as exotic as all Byzantium, the head of a woman, so realistic, so direct. Defying time and the wreckage all around, four female figures in flowing robes span the Hall of Virtues, where the humanist scholar János Vitéz had his study. They personify the four virtues—and the charm, the balance and the serenity of Hungary's Renaissance at its height.

Down by the riverside, the Primate's Palace stands its ground. The Museum of Christian Art is sheltered here, its running costs subsidized by the state. Two nineteenth-century prelates collected the art works and objects on display—Hungarian and Italian first and foremost; German, Austrian, Dutch and Flemish, too. In the quiet of mid-day, I approach the huge, heavy doors to the museum and enter a rarified world of saints and martyrs and mysticism. The *Lord's Coffin* is drawn up in front of me, a ceremonial coffin of gilded wood, carved by an unknown hand. Wheeled along on a symbolic bier, it served as a prop in the passion play staged during Holy Week in Garamszentbenedek, a town now in Czechoslovakia. Ranged around the coffin are the twelve disciples, their features modelled after townsfolk who took part in the production five centuries ago. St. James has a furrowed brow and dark, heavy hair. St. Andrew is fair with flaccid cheeks. The roof of the coffin bristles with pinnacles and pointed arches; moving scenes of Christ's passion decorate the bier. Theatrical in conception, the *Lord's Coffin* is profoundly spiritual as well. It is a relic from an earlier age of faith.

The *Calvary Altarpiece* from the Benedictine Abbey of Garamszentbenedek was painted in the year 1427 by one Tamás of Kolosvár, a man of passion and rare sensibility. Tamás of Kolosvár: barely known to outsiders, perhaps. But a painter to be reckoned with. The central panel shows Christ on the cross bending towards a swooning Virgin, her long, slender hands limp with grief. So much emotion, so much despair are drawn out under a sky of Gothic gold. How different the scene of resurrection. Framed in an aureole, Christ floats gently out of his grave, the son of God in a body divine. In a new century another master reinvented the language of anguish and of joy: the master who signed himself merely M.S. His *Calvary* of 1506 hangs in the gloom of an adjoining gallery. A museum guard rushes on ahead to activate the push-button lighting system, revealing the altarpiece, a lurid crimson and veridian. In terrible torment, this crucified Christ suffers the full measure of his agony. Resurrected, he ascends to even greater bliss.

Halfway between Budapest and the Balaton lies Székesfehérvár. An industrial suburb surrounds the old town centre—Hungary's oldest town centre—medieval Alba Regia, sovereign city of the Hungarian crown. It is a timeless place and magical, too, by all accounts. Yet the bleak streets of the new city reach right up to the historic precinct, and I hardly dare hope for enchantment. You can drive into the old quarter, but most people go on foot. Mothers push streamlined prams with plastic peep-holes. Children pedal furiously along on bikes. They head into Szabadság

Fertőd: a palace of Baroque
magnificence, Hungary's Versailles.

Guardians of the arts keep an
eye on Vasarely's Op art
geometrics and Munkácsy's
illusionist effects.

Square, heedless of the Garden of Ruins off to one side, with its scattering of stones. The stones mark the site of Alba Regia's Basilica and coronation church, demolished by the Turks and long since grown over with grass. St. Stephen was buried in this hallowed ground—interred in the Roman sarcophagus that is kept under cover of a nearby arcade, visible for all to see. A Hungarian sculptor embellished the bare marble for the obsequies of the king; rosettes in Romanesque style frame the winged angels that saw St. Stephen into the grave.

I cross Szabadság Square with its Baroque stuccowork and tile and enter the pedestrian zone of Március 15 Street. Székesfehérvár is out in its thousands, propelling me along. The caretakers of the Pharmacy Museum in the street wear uniforms and adopt a confusing professional air. Standing beside carved wood display cases, they seem all too ready to dispense the drugs that fill matching glass apothecary jars, labelled in Latin and lavished with ornamental scrolls. Outside again, I follow the human cavalcade as it drifts off into the warren of streets that curves back towards Szabadság Square. In these streets are little shops that have barely changed in half a century, or one or two: a harness makers', smelling of leather, gleaming with brass, a jewellers' selling oddments, a cosmeticians' veiled in lace. And so on all the way back to Szabadság Square. Beyond is the Gothic Church of St. Anne and Székesfehérvár's Baroque cathedral. Then more little streets, more little shops, an enclave within an enclave, a world within a world.

Pannonhalma is a city, too, a city of God. The Benedictine monastery defends the "Sacred Mountain of Pannonia" now as it has for a thousand years. The century-old dome of the abbey church looms large above me as I go up the hillside, blanketed in trees. Besieged by the Mongols, overrun by the Turks, Pannonhalma survives in Neo-classical guise. You have to join a group to visit the monastic complex, the church, the cloister and the library. Into the ancient crypt trail the crowds and out the medieval Porta Speciosa into the cloister. Sunlight filters through stained-glass medallions; there is an aura of holiness and history here. The library, a gilt-and-grey marble monument of Neo-classical decoration, preserves precious documents of the Hungarian nation: the charter of Pannonhalma itself, signed by St. Stephen in the first year of the eleventh century, and the deed of Tihany Abbey, the first document to use words in the Hungarian language. The library shelves sag under the weight of hundreds of thousands of volumes. No Benedictine library is larger. Peace lies on this place and the light of learning.

In Győr it will always be Saturday for me. There are people everywhere, the people of Győr. People with market baskets and bulging plastic bags. People with parcels tied up in string. People, a constant stream of people, flood into Győr's inner city, thronging the shops, the cafés, the stands of the outdoor market. This Saturday—every Saturday—Győr pulses with life. The crowds fall away as I go up to the cathedral, founded by St. Stephen, burned out by the Turks. There are Rococo pews and Neo-classical pillars. There is the promise of heaven on the ceiling overhead, a heaven teeming with angels and cherubim. One look from St. László could command that heavenly host. The saint's features, his powerful nose and penetrating eyes, are immortalized in the Gothic reliquary bust of Héderváry Chapel—a formidable characterization, formidably executed—a masterpiece of the Hungarian goldsmith's art.

Roofs of tile sag against the sky in Sopron. Cobbles pave the streets. Traffic does not penetrate the hidden precincts of the inner city, drowsing in the red and blue of weathered paint. I hear distant voices, the sound of footsteps in the street. Sopron lies like a dream all around me, as day dissolves into night. A wedding party files past, led by a bride in white. Bride and well-wishers walk on into the dusk, participants in an ancient rite. Sopron is a perfect medieval city, preserved in all its purity. Neither the Mongols nor the Turks reached this distant town in the foothills of Austria's Alps. Most of the houses are in Gothic style; a few rise on Roman foundations. For Sopron is the Scarbantia of the Romans and as old as the empire itself. Eggenberger House has shadowy Gothic courtyards. Erdődy Palace is encrusted with Rococo reliefs. Fabricius House in the main square, Fő tér, stands on Roman underpinnings. Patches of damp stain the ancient inner court, a maze of passageways and staircases, and a museum of Roman finds lurks in one of the cellars. Across the way is a vintage pharmacy and the Gothic cathedral, the Goat Church, built by a goatherd and blazoned with goats. Steep stone steps lead below the level of the square to a wine cellar. I stop here to drink a brimming glassful of *Soproni kékfrankos*, Sopron's clear red wine, a wine redolent of ancient revelries. Beyond the cellar, beyond the square stretch the streets of the inner city. I set off through those silent streets, tracing the horseshoe-shaped outlines of Scarbantia. And the twentieth century fades with the light.

When Queen Maria Theresa sat on the throne, Miklós Eszterházy held sway at Fertőd, a palace of Baroque magnificence, Hungary's Versailles. Time and the ravages of war have taken their toll. But Fertőd stands fast, the very symbol of princely power, the power of a prince of the Holy

"If the earth is God's hat,
then Hungary's the bouquet
on that..."
Sándor Petőfi

Every age finds something
to enjoy.

Roman Empire. Joseph Haydn was musician in residence, and Haydn's music still echoes in the concert hall, a venue for summer performances. Ormolu, faience, lacquer and marble decorate the Sala Terrena, the Chinese Room, the salons—rooms full of majesty and of poignancy. Most visitors make their way through the enfilade of rooms in an hour or less, and I do not linger longer. I prefer to sit out in the courtyard, looking up at that remarkable façade, so compelling in the rhythm of its sweeping curves.

The name of Ferenc Rákóczi II and his legendary fame bring me to the eastern reaches of Hungary, to Sárospatak, the Rákóczi seat. My fascination with Rákóczi began when I happened on a reproduction of the stunning portrait by Ádám Mányoki that hangs in the Hungarian National Gallery. Rákóczi sat for the picture in 1712, the year after he lost the fight for Hungarian independence (and possession of Sárospatak). Defeated but not abashed, he looks out from the canvas, a romantic figure with free-flowing hair, sensual lips, clear eyes. He faces the blows of life squarely, wrapped in the dignity of a resplendent scarlet cloak. Two and a half centuries on, the memory of Hungary's great patriot and revolutionary remains vividly alive. Hungarians still lay wreaths and roses on his shrine at Sárospatak—and no withered blossoms these.

I pull up to the castle under a glowering sky. It looks grand and grey and gloomy with the knowledge of so many charged events. Antal Pálóczi left Sárospatak to fight the Turks at Mohács. He died in battle and never saw the castle again. Gábor Perényi, a supporter of the Reformation, fled Sárospatak under attack by royal forces. During the ill-fated War of Independence, Ferenc Rákóczi convened Hungary's diet here, defying the Habsburgs as his father had done a generation earlier. The first Ferenc Rákóczi narrowly escaped with his life when his bid to liberate Hungary failed. The conspiracy he joined was plotted under the stucco rose of Sárospatak's Sub Rosa room. On entering the castle, I head straight for this room, unchanged after more than three hundred years. The famous rose still hugs the ceiling overhead, carved when Hungary was in bondage to Austria, struggling to break free. The rooms beyond commemorate the life and times of the younger Rákóczi, who died in exile in Turkey, bereft of Sárospatak and so far from this place.

Rain pelts down as I dash across the muddy courtyard to the medieval keep. Chill, white-washed rooms with arched Gothic ceilings and sumptuous Renaissance decoration testify to a world in transition, the world of the troubadour Bálint Balassi, who courted the ravishing Krisztina Dobó here. Linked to the keep, the superb Late Renaissance

Opposite and overleaf: three faces of Hungary's Eve.

76

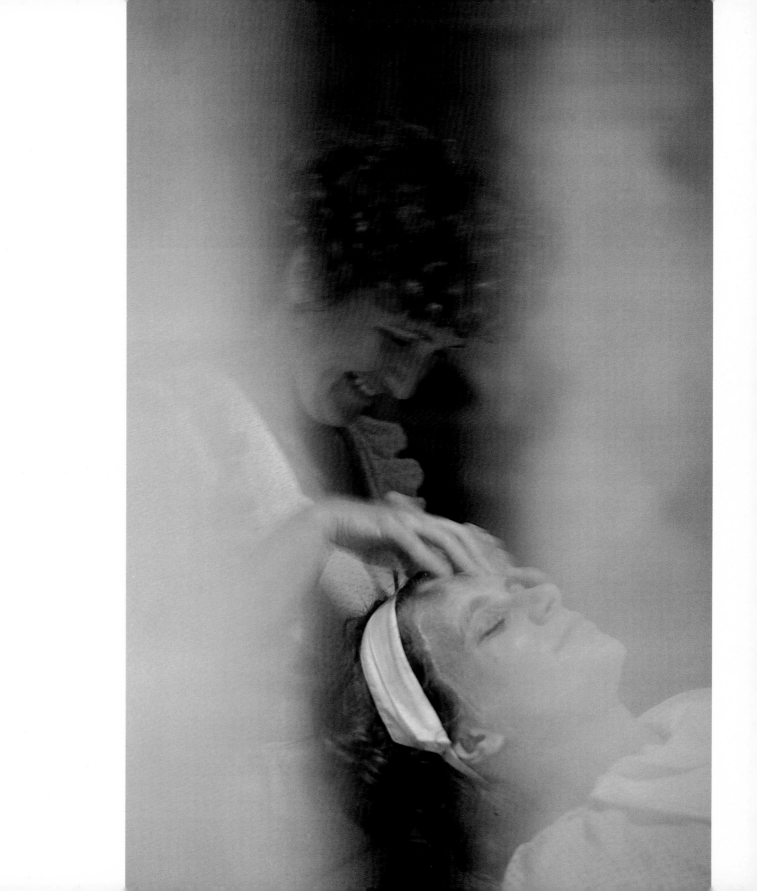

Nothing about Hungary impressed
me more than the people.

Hungary has all the monuments a
momentous past provides.

Many here are religious, too.

Hungary's cities hold the historical
monuments of the nation in store.

"Clay is my daily bread, my joy and my sorrow", Margit Kovács declared.

Lorántffy Gallery is less pure in style but noble nonetheless. At the time of its construction—and throughout the Turkish occupation—Sárospatak remained independent, a bastion of the Renaissance and of the Reformation.

Revolution and Reformation follow me south to Debrecen, the "Calvinist Rome", where central squares bear the names of Calvin and Kossuth, Lajos Kossuth, leader of the nineteenth-century independence movement. In the troubled year of 1849 Kossuth called Hungary's Parliament to Debrecen, where members voted to overthrow the Habsburgs. They met in the Calvinist Great Church, a monument of history and of religion, uncompromising in its Neo-classical architecture, unbending in its faith. After a quick look at this forbidding place of worship, I abandon the austerities of Calvinism for the blandishments of the Déri Museum, founded by Frigyes Déri, a Hungarian-born entrepreneur of Austrian descent. Single-minded, undeterred by Egyptian mummy cases and Chinese robes, I make for the Art Gallery and the collection of pictures by Mihály Munkácsy.

A great painter, perhaps Hungary's greatest painter, Munkácsy was as much at home in a bourgeois milieu as in the company of peasants. He was versatile and prolific, turning his hand to portraiture, landscape, historical and religious subjects, to the themes of everyday life. Although the National Gallery in Budapest claims the lion's share of works, the Déri Museum displays fewer pictures to greater advantage. Like the sympathetic portrayal of an outlaw at table, ever vigilant, never at ease. And the urbane study of an arch young woman, confident of her charms. But the monumental *Ecce Homo* takes pride of place. This stridently realistic scene reverberates with pathos: scorned, Christ stands before the crowd, no more than a man, no less than a king.

Debrecen is the third city of Hungary, preceded only by Budapest and industrial Miskolc. There are so many cities. I have so little time—just time enough for Kecskemét, fragrant with apricots, renowned for its brandy. And for Pécs with its mosques and minaret. For Szeged on the Tisza, a city of bridges and boulevards. And for Siklós with its castle. So many cities and no two alike. So many proud cities of Hungary.

TRADITIONS

While Hungary's cities hold the historical monuments of the nation in store, the villages safeguard the traditions, the arts—the very soul of the people. Hungary has thousands of villages; Galgamácsa is one. Trucks rattle down the dusty main street. High fences hide the houses from view. Thirty miles from Budapest, I leave the capital far behind me. For Galgamácsa. For the village.

A young man lets me into the courtyard of a house within hailing distance of the general store and café. Hungary's foremost folk painter, Juli Dudás, appears, dressed in a peasant skirt and kerchief. A small woman, still beautiful in her early sixties, she has remarkable slanting eyes, fine bones, delicate hands. She leads me into the sitting room, decked with plates she painted herself: there is no mistaking the meticulous style and peasant subject matter. On the wall hang photographs of the artist with her mentor, Zoltán Kodály, Hungary's great composer and music educator. Juli Dudás was no more than "five or six years when some strangers, who seemed like two strolling players, made me sing at the well where I tended my geese". The strangers were Kodály and his friend Béla Bartók. In the twenties and thirties the two "village travellers" went from one isolated community to another, recording the songs of Hungary's peasants on a gramophone, preserving the words and music for all time.

As Juli Dudás matured, Kodály encouraged her to sketch, to sing, to collect traditional songs. She began to paint seriously and her reputation grew as her talent developed, leading to important exhibitions in Hungary and abroad. Named Master of Folk Art in 1956, Juli Dudás has travelled far from Galgamácsa, but she has never forsaken her peasant identity. Nor has her art ever strayed from the themes of village life. She chronicles the labours, the seasons, the customs of old Galgamácsa: Easter Monday "sprinkling", for example, when boys doused girls with water from the well. The fire-leaping competition held on St. John's Day in June. Social gatherings in the spinning room.

Kalocsa embroidery blooms with the pink, blue, yellow and lavender of meadow flowers.

Juli Dudás glorifies Galgamácsa, the Galgamácsa of her childhood, the Galgamácsa of her imagination. And Galgamácsa has honoured Juli Dudás, founding a museum in her name, an old stucco-and-thatch dwelling where the best of her art is displayed in a homely setting. Not only do the pictures document village life, but they also stand on their own as accomplished masterworks, vibrant with colour and emotion. In the portrayal of a wedding feast, the artist takes obvious delight in the minutiae of dress and demeanour. While it is the inexorable movement of the figures that concerns her in the Christmas Night procession. Shown in profile, the villagers proceed in ranks like an advancing army. Even the stiff points of the women's heavy black shawls stir into motion, echoing the cadence of marching feet. Through the winter snow the villagers go, keeping step on up to the little yellow church of Galgamácsa.

And to the east lies Zsámbok. Not every map of Hungary situates the village. Not every foreigner makes his way here. Zsámbok is quiet, unexceptional—drab, even. Until the sun sinks in the sky, sheathing Zsámbok in its gold. And dust blows off the dusk streets. Then Zsámbok lies transformed, ready for the rites of its peasant bride. Today and every day a girl of the village is to "marry": tourists attend the festivities as "guests". Aunt Margit, the village matriarch, oversees preparations. I meet up with her in the Zsámbok museum—a typical house of stucco and thatch—as she rushes about in a frenzy of last-minute tidying. Perspiration beads her lip, and her grey hair curls out from under an embroidered coif, refusing to be subdued. She wears a red cashmere skirt in the old style and a white blouse with red and green embroidery that is "really too frivolous" for a woman in her sixties, she says. Childless, widowed young, remarried only in middle age, this vital woman has devoted all her energies to the museum. Her own collection of peasant clothing and artefacts forms the core of museum holdings, and she went on to solicit many articles more. "Everything is vanishing", Aunt Margit exclaims, as she pulls heavy silk shawls, pleated skirts and embroidered sheepskin jackets out of drawers to show me. "So much has been lost", she continues, fingering the rich old materials lovingly. Some of the pieces belonged to her mother and to her grandmother before that. A rising generation possesses them now.

The wedding participants assemble and the tourists arrive—a small group transported by bus from Budapest. Aunt Margit leaves me to welcome them, and the wedding spectacular begins. Acting as master of ceremonies, the best man leads us out through the sunset streets of Zsámbok. Gypsy violins play. The bridal party paces solemnly along,

100

bedizened with pearls and ribbon. They sing traditional songs; the bride chants farewell to her parents. Stoical villagers feign tears. And it's on to the feast and the dancing.

There are no tears at a real peasant wedding, I discover. Nor songs of farewell (though certain traditions survive). There is a sense of community, of celebration. On a farm just south of Décs, a village of the southern Sárköz region, preparations for a wedding feast are underway one fine Saturday morning. In the yard a team of cooks cuts up chickens for soup and mutton for stew, piling the meat into mountains. Huge cauldrons simmer fiendishly on portable outdoor cookers. A band strikes up, testing out its amplifiers. The band is here for the duration, and so are the guests; everyone will eat lunch and dinner together. The wedding ceremony itself is to take place at the Décs registry office in the afternoon. The bride will wear white, donning her peasant costume at midnight for the traditional "bride's dance", when—as custom decrees—her partners pay for the privilege of a dance. The proceeds can be considerable.

I make to go as more guests arrive, but the bride's mother implores, "Stay, stay. You haven't seen the pastries". And with that she shepherds me into the kitchen, where dozens of cakes are stored: chocolate cakes, strawberry cakes, cakes coated with pink and white sugar, cakes enough to give away as presents to all the wedding guests. Again I try to take my leave, but the family choruses, "Don't go away yet. You haven't met the bride". After a while, she drives up in a truck—blasé, barely twenty, all of life before her. Later, in Décs, the wedding party speeds past me on the way to the civil ceremony. Everybody toots and waves. It is blazing hot and the village falls back into silence. If it is true that the bride on whom the sun shines will be happy, that girl is bound for a life of bliss.

The imposing town houses of Décs decay genteelly in the sun, their woodwork bleached a mottled pink, blue and green. Little Ionic columns, fat as cigars, adorn white stucco façades. A century old, the houses date from the era of legendary prosperity that followed drainage of the Sárköz swamps. The sun bears down mercilessly as I walk to the old house given over to the village museum and handicraft cooperative. A dusty tree casts its shade now and then. The museum is open, empty. Built on an "L", this spacious dwelling has bourgeois pretensions; nonetheless its peasant origins are clear. Here, as in every venerable peasant dwelling, a ceremonial bed stands in the best room. No one ever slept in this bed-of-state: draped with hand-embroidered covers and stacked with duvets, it symbolized the wealth and standing of the household. Tinted photographs of upright villagers line the walls, and multi-colour rag rugs lie

I knock at the door of a wizened old lady, stooped and small.

Zsámbok's peasant brides are
bedizened with pearls and ribbon.

Herdsmen of Hortobágy revive
the old life of the plain.

He could be a factory worker or a mechanic—but for his staff and his sense of vocation.

underfoot, while the dark, painted furniture and pottery echo the opulence of the gentry that was. Women throughout the region embroider the articles offered for sale in the shop alongside, operated by the local cooperative. Traditionally, Sárköz work features field flowers and the colour yellow—and in these parts traditions count.

The needlewomen of Mezőkövesd, a northern village, perpetuate the rose-and-tulip motif of the Matyó region, adapting venerable patterns to modern uses. For the embroidery of Mezőkövesd and the hamlets all around has ancestral renown. The Matyó museum in the House of Culture glows darkly with jewel colour and dazzling silk thread. The *matyók* raised embroidery to a high art, clothing themselves in their most ornate creations. The finest work dates from the first three decades of the century. Pearls, sequins and braid gilded the lily—until the village priest banned such sumptuous apparel in the twenties and ordered it burned.

As for the women of Kalocsa, they have difficulty keeping up with the demand for their floral embroidery, or so Antalné Szvétek says. A Master of Folk Art, this skilled craftswoman is also versed in the daubed mural painting of old Kalocsa. Every surface of her modern house blooms with the pink, blue, yellow and lavender of meadow flowers. For our meeting, Mrs. Szvétek sports intricately stitched garb, complete with lacy cap and apron, but she confesses that she would not dream of wearing the costume every day. It is just too difficult to launder, to starch and to iron.

All the same, clotheslines in Hollókő flap with cream linen blouses, embroidered around the sleeves with clusters of roses, red and blue; for roses grow in profusion in this Palóc village, spilling over garden fences and scenting the air. Most of the women here dress in time-honoured style. You see them striding out to the fields in those blouses, in sweeping skirts and colourful knitted waistcoats. Or walking along the roadway past Hungary's most picturesque village houses—houses washed in white paint and roofed in tile, windows flung open on the world. Up at the museum, the caretaker sits out on the verandah embroidering. She takes pride in comparing the quality of her work with that of the textiles on display inside. Further along, a woman calls out with embroidery to sell. But I knock at the door of a wizened old lady, stooped and small. Her eyesight failing, she sews no more, though once her needlework was the equal of any in the village. She bids me enter, gathering up examples of her artistry: tablecloths, petticoats, blouses. A widow in black, the old lady has no use for these embroidered pieces. Her husband is long gone and all her children, too. She agrees to let me buy a blouse, one of her own linen blouses, to wear "in happiness and health".

LEISURE

Béla Farkas plays for himself first. But he also plays for me. From the heart, with feeling. One of Hungary's great gypsy musicians, he is a poet of the violin. I ask to hear the old songs, the timeless pieces of Bihari and Dankó. And Béla Farkas begins, improvising a concert the likes of which I'll never hear again. I forget the hotel dining room where I sit and the people around me. There is no one but Béla Farkas, nothing but those extraordinary hands — hands that cradle the violin and are all but fused to it — phrasing Pista Dankó's exquisite airs: *Silence, My Sweetheart, Silence, Silence, One Cat, Two Cats, My Violin was Broken.* This last song, the most moving of the four hundred or more Dankó composed, can easily ring false. But Béla Farkas plays without sentimentality or artifice, exalting the tune in its simplicity.

He brings the same purity to his interpretation of János Bihari's *I Love You, I Love You, I Love You,* and *I'm Out of My Mind,* songs popular for nearly two hundred years. And when Béla Farkas bows the *Spur Verbunk,* a recruiting tune, the legendary magnetism attributed to these rollicking melodies actually becomes credible. They were designed to lure peasants into the grips of army recruitment officers. Plied with wine while the music played on, the peasants usually joined up without realizing it, signing years and years of their lives away.

From the gypsy tradition Béla Farkas turns to the Hungarian repertoire, performing classics like *Acacia Road,* written at the turn of the century, and *I Asked It of a Flower.* These songs have a haunting, melancholy quality and a rhythm more measured than that of the gypsy tunes. The sincerity of execution plainly inspires the other members of the group, the cellist, the cymbalom player, the violinists.

During breaks in the playing, Béla Farkas speaks about his music, his life. It is no surprise to hear that music is his life. Taught both by his father and his grandfather, he began to study the violin at the age of six. By twelve, he was leader of a group. Many awards followed. No believer in alcohol, he sips a glass of water as we talk, claiming that his fingers "move less well" if he drinks. Béla Farkas maintains that there will always be a place for gypsy music, despite the fact that changing tastes and a changing public have put the future somewhat into question. He admits that musicians of the new generation are soon counted and that there are fewer groups—and smaller—than ever before. Nevertheless he looks on the continuing creation of songs as a hopeful sign.

His son, who acts as *primas*, or lead violinist, of the group, feels differently. Married, with a small son of his own, the younger Béla Farkas has no intention of encouraging the boy to follow in his footsteps. He can see his son as a classical violinist, if he shows talent, but not as a gypsy player. The gypsy tradition is dying out, he says. By way of reply, the elder Béla Farkas strikes up the *Rákóczi March*, the standard finale, and he plays the piece that originally gained currency during the eighteenth-century War of Independence as if for the first time, as if for all time.

Wave after wave of ardent applause floods the Budapest Sports Hall as Árpád Joó lays down his baton. He has just led the Budapest Symphony Orchestra in a matchless performance of Mahler's *Eighth Symphony,* televised nationally and recorded for release by Hungaroton, the state record company. The only venue expansive enough to hold the massed choirs of "The Symphony of a Thousand", the stadium is full up. And so is the Academy of Music when János Ferencsik conducts the Hungarian State Symphony Orchestra. And when the Liszt Ferenc Chamber Orchestra plays, and the Bartók String Quartet. Hungarians have a passion for music, the Hungarian classics above all: the rhapsodies and sonatas of Liszt, the lyrical operas of Ferenc Erkel, the works of Béla Bartók and Zoltán Kodály. Kodály's experimental methods of music education have a great deal to do with it. The Kodály approach has influenced the tastes of three generations, fostering an appreciation of folk forms first and, by extension, all others.

You can actually feel the presence of Kodály at Buda's Youth Park, where young people meet two evenings a week to learn the old dances of Hungary and neighbouring countries. They practice the steps in animated groups of twenty or more—turning, kicking, keeping time to the amplified music that comes crackling over loudspeakers. At the former Buda casino —home theatre of the Hungarian State Folk Ensemble—more dancers whirl and stomp. They are accomplished amateurs from Debrecen, in the capital for a series of special performances. Some of the troupe are secondary school students, others young workers; all are excited by the idea of appearing in Budapest. They normally play provincial houses of

These streets were made for walking and that is what I do.

118

There will always be a place
for gypsy music.

culture or trade union headquarters, a young carpenter says. A member of the troupe for eleven years, he is the oldest at twenty-nine. And he has no intention of dropping out. He likes the sense of participation the dancing gives him, the sheer athleticism, the link with the past. Inspired by the music, the lights, the audience, this young man performs with total abandon, expressing the very joy of living as he bounds across the stage.

City Park is the scene of a country-and-western concert, held on the Day of the Child. The "100 Folk Celsius" group (the name is a play on the Hungarian work *fok,* meaning "degrees") takes to the platform. Dressed in workaday denims—nothing theatrical, nothing flashy—they interpret the Nashville sound for an enthusiastic following, performing old hits like *Down by the Banks of the Ohio.* On the second run-through, the crowd joins in, shouting out the word "Ohio" with gusto. The group also has success with songs of their own composing: *Asphalt Country in Great Budapest, Housing Estate, Give it to Him Boy.* Five members strong, "100 Folk Celsius" say they like country music because it is "easy and relaxed". They may joke about their unique "red grass" style, but their singing carries real conviction.

Lights burn low in the Rondella. People come here to drink, to talk, to revel in "the big dream of Budapest by night", as the poet Endre Ady phrased it. Wine is essential to the celebration. Tamás Dózsa, manager of the establishment, measures it in thousands of litres: five thousand sold every month, sixty thousand every year. Half of all those thousands is red, a quarter, dry white and the rest, sweet white wine. All of it is Hungarian. "There is a patriotism in the wine, too, you know", one man says. "For us, the Hungarians, Hungarian wine is best." Tamás Dózsa stocks nothing else.

He fills five little glasses with five different wines, explaining that Hungarian wines are produced by state farms, by cooperatives and by private individuals. Shipping companies bottle a limited amount for export. He urges me to try the first wine, *Soproni kékfrankos,* a light red from the western wine-growing region of Sopron, bordering on Austria. And I take a sip of the frank *Kékfrankos.* It is a strong wine for strong foods like beef and game, Tamás Dózsa says. Hungarians often mix it with soda water. They add soda to *Csopaki Olaszrizling,* too. This white is a typical table wine, he continues, an accompaniment to pork, fish and chicken. And I taste the wine of Csopak, a Balaton wine, fresh, fruity, fugitive. *Badacsonyi szürkebarát* also comes from the Balaton. The name means "Grey Monk". Hungarians call this wine their "grey friend" because it is neither dry nor sweet, neither black nor white. So I sample the heady

The Balaton: Central Europe's
largest lake, Hungary's sea.

Szürkebarát. This wine goes well with pancakes, strudels and cakes. The fourth glass contains six-year-old *Tokaji szamorodni.* Hungarians reserve this dry white wine for special occasions, drinking it as an aperitif or with cheese. And I savour the *Szamorodni,* not a dry wine by my lights, but warming, vigorous. The fifth glass brims with sweet *Tokaji aszu,* eight years old. Like the *Szamorodni,* the *Aszu* is a wine for high days and holy days. I quaff the golden *Aszu,* the most intoxicating wine of all. Then Tamás Dózsa produces one last glass, pouring out a tot of brandy, Hungarian apricot brandy, distilled from the fruit of Kecskemét. And with my brandy I drink to the health of Tamás Dózsa and to the people of Hungary, to all the good people of Hungary.

German drinking songs resound in the wine cellars of Hajós—situated out in the vineyards, at one remove from the village proper. Virtually every Hajós family has its cellar and its vines. The oldest cellars date from the turn of the eighteenth century, when settlers from the South German Duchy of Swabia made their way here. Subsequent waves of Swabians reinforced links between villagers and their former homeland, and even now well over half the population is Swabian and German-speaking. The thousand or more cellars of Hajós line rutted dirt lanes. Planted side by side, one after another, the diminutive buildings look like elfin dwellings of a storybook town. Old men haunt the place. One of them beckons—a patriarchal figure with cropped white hair and gnarled fingers. He rinses a filmy glass in cold water, filling it with a sparkling wine of his own making, rose pale and refreshing. Like the other villagers, he keeps the wine for his own use, sharing it freely with the strangers who come his way. Further along, another man offers his white wine, blended from a selection of the five or six varieties of grape that grow in Hajós. In one of the newer cellars dating from the twenties or thirties, a group of young footballers fraternize. They are finishing off the remains of *pince-pörkölt,* or cellar stew, a classic dish containing pork, cooked over a smouldering wood fire. They set me down in their midst and there I stay, drinking the afternoon away with those hale fellows, well met.

You eat well at the Híd, an old inn of Óbuda, and "Schrammel" music plays. Or so says a Budapest friend, as we set off for the restaurant. Óbuda lies in darkness. The Híd blazes with light. There is noise and a crowd and the pungent odour of meat roasting, baking, grilling. Reputed for more than a century, the kitchen maintains its good name. Grilled steak has long been a speciality. It was the favourite dish of the novelist Gyula Krudy, who frequented the Híd at the turn of the century. A plaque on the wall commemorates Krudy the gastronome, the writer who loved to eat. We order and we eat: paprika-laden steak tartare, piquant in the Hungarian style. A fiery red wine. Pig's knuckle, cooked to perfection, leaner and meatier than in Germany. And crisp strudel, filled with sugared sour cherries, that delectable Hungarian fruit. All through the meal, the "Schrammel" band plays, the accordion and violin rousing the crowd with old Austrian airs. They play louder and faster as the night wears on. And everybody dances, everybody sings.

The Híd is a monument. Hungary has more: the inn at Hortobágy renowned for its mutton stew. And the terrace restaurant overlooking the Balaton that specializes in giant pike-perch, fresh from the lake. The hotel dining room in Eger, where they serve goulash soup in little metal cauldrons. And Gundel's, the old Budapest establishment, named after Károly Gundel. The Escoffier of Hungary, he codified the cuisine of the country in a cookery book that has gone through countless editions. Kálmán Kozma, maître d'hôtel of Gundel's, describes Hungary's unique and varied cuisine. First, he points out, the tradition for soups is strong, be it fish, bean or chicken soup, or one of the cold fruit preparations. Pork and organ meats—especially liver—figure prominently, and most foods are cooked in lard. Paprika provides soups and sauces with colour, flavour and consistency. To extract the full flavour, the powder is stirred into melted lard. The other ingredients are added quickly to prevent heat from souring the spice and destroying its effect. Caraway seed, marjoram and dill season many dishes. Garlic is used lightly. Sour cream is important, and so is a basic sauce of lard, tomato, onion and green pepper known as *lecsó*. Vegetables are nearly always prepared in the Hungarian style, with a sauce of lard, flour and vegetable stock.

Hungary's greatest invention, *pörkölt* or stew, originated with the shepherds of the Great Plain, Kálmán Kozma continues. They simply combined the meat of the animals around them with lard, onions and paprika. As for sweets, he concludes, Hungarians never tire of strudel—whether the plum and apple varieties or cabbage, pumpkin and poppy seed. Submerged in custard, cream and chocolate, Somló sponge cake proves another favourite, as do the pancakes for which Gundel's is famous. The invention of Károly Gundel himself, they are drenched in a rich rum and chocolate sauce. Tall, trim and athletic, Kálmán Kozma nevertheless succumbs to temptation, exercizing excess calories away. Not so every Hungarian: truth be told, the national silhouette tends towards pleasing plumpness.

The table is set for thirty. I take my place near the head. Wild boar is in the offing, shot by the men seated all around me. Baja's best marksmen,

Parachuting into People's
Stadium...

...where women dominate the field.

they are paid-up members of the Hungarian National Hunter's Society, celebrating the end of yet another satisfying season. The hunters are gathered out of doors, in a clearing a stone's throw from their rustic clubhouse. Corn fields and forests stretch near and far. Boar stew simmers in a cauldron over a gas flame. The recipe is simple, the cook avers, as he ladles a generous helping into my bowl. You take the fresh meat of half a boar and cut it into chunks.... Laced with lard and paprika, the stew is rich and peppery. The hunters mop up the thick gravy with pieces of crusty bread, helping themselves to pickles now and then. I follow suit, keeping up with those hearty appetites: one bowl, two bowls, three bowls, four. And just as many glasses of foamy red wine, mixed with soda from a siphon.

Hungary's spas offer one of life's great sybaritic experiences.

As we eat, the men talk about their favourite sport. The season just past was good, they say, but national preservation laws are strict. The number of animals and the species that can be killed change from year to year. The hunters stalk deer, ram and boar. In fields they use the watch towers that stand alongside the clubhouse. This minimizes damage to crops, damage that can run to millions of forints a year nationwide. They keep two guns, one for blanks, another for bullets—and a prescribed amount of ammunition. Straight shooting, they observe, is a natural aptitude. The president of the Baja club adds that reflexes are "in the veins". One man claims he started shooting at the age of ten; another was thirteen, a third, seventeen. All were taught by their fathers. Unanimously, they declare that the English are the world's best hunters—after the Hungarians, of course.

While tens of thousands of Hungarians belong to the National Hunter's Society, far fewer are affiliated with the various flying clubs of Hungary. What they lack in numbers, they make up in enthusiasm for gliders like the Góbé, designed by a Rubik, father of Ernő of cube and puzzle fame. At an airfield south of Budapest, I meet a young Malév pilot who indulges his passion for flying off duty as well as on. Gliders excite him just as much as conventional airplanes, he says, looking over at a Góbé beached on the grass, red-and-yellow paintwork gleaming, bubble hatch snapped down. The success of a glider flight is measured either in distance pure and simple, or in distance and time, the pilot explains. Apart from the Góbé, the club has other, streamlined planes. Members mill around, helping to launch the gliders and watching them land. Waiting for a turn in the air, they live life on the wing.

Riding has its own thrills, I discover at Bugac. Out in the puszta, champions stage an incomparable exhibition of equestrian skills. There is no horse-ring, nor stands for spectators. Just endless plain and sky and the

136

nónius horses of the Lenin cooperative. Riders put the horses through their paces, walking, trotting, galloping, drawing carriages. They urge their mounts to lie down while they sit atop them, cracking their whips, demonstrating the evasory tactics used by the one-time outlaws of the plain. Parallel to the ground, the horses were invisible to oncoming riders. Accustomed by the crack of the whip to the report of gunfire, they were impervious to fear. In a display of daredevil riding, a horseman drives a team of five from a standing position atop the bare backs of the two animals that bring up the rear, one foot on each careering horse. Then the stud flies past, unfettered, riderless, free. The thundering hooves throw up a trail of dust and with it an image of the old life of the plain.

And so on to a thermal bath. Hungary's spas offer one of life's great sybaritic experiences, cognoscenti tell me. Most guides and brochures give short shrift to the sheer hedonism of it all, they say, packing me off to Budapest's Gellért establishment, an art deco pleasure palace of 1918 with separate but equal facilities for men and women. Everything about the place is grandiose, from the entrance hall with its cathedral ceiling, marble columns and Grecian statuary to the vaulted thermal pools themselves, faced in ornamental tile. In the changing room, an attendant hands out rubber scuffs and bath sheets. She points to the shower and the thermal pools, where a cross-section of Hungarian womanhood soaks, bare flesh rippling, impressive unclothed. I take the plunge and try to swim, but the heat inhibits movement, inducing a state of blissful lethargy. From time to time, I clamber out for a drink of mineral water from one of the enormous marble fountains—only to collapse into hot water again, only to fall back into a trance. The baths provoke a curious feeling of detachment and buoyancy: there are no windows, there is no harsh lighting, there is nothing but tile, humidity and hot water. I come out of that bath invigorated and changed somehow, changed for the better.

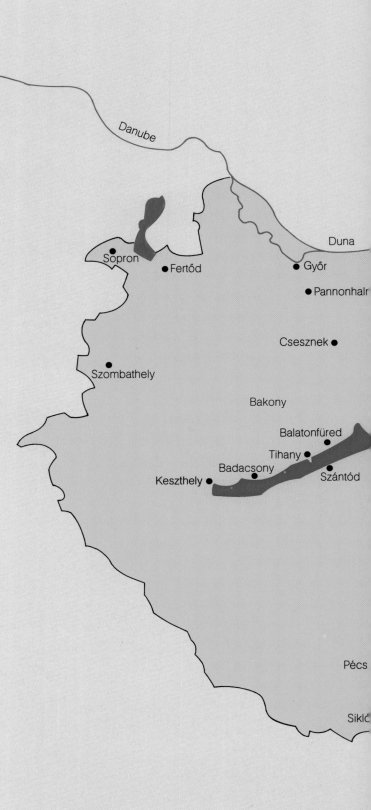

Acknowledgments
We wish to express our thanks to Vue Touristique I.P.V.,
Budapest and in particular to Professor Joseph J. Hollos
for initiating and seeing this book through.

Typeset and printed by Weber S.A., Bienne
Lithos: Gravor S.A., Bienne
Bound by Mayer & Soutter S.A., Renens